CIAO BAMBINO!

Acknowledgement:
For my "be anything you can dream" mom,
who inspired me to write again.
- Danna

First published by AuthorHouse 01/10/05

ISBN: 1-4208-0082-5 (sc)

Library of Congress Control Number: 2004098056

Printed in the United States of America
Bloomington, Indiana

This book is printed on acid-free paper.

www.ciaobambinobooks.com

CIAO BAMBINO!

A Child's Tour of Italy

BY **Danna Troncatty Leahy**

ILLUSTRATED BY **Gabhor Utomo**

www.ciaobambinobooks.com

AuthorHouse Publishing

Ciao Bambino!

Guess where I have been?

I went on a special trip with

Mommy and Daddy.

We took a family vacation to Italy. Italy is a country in Europe far from home. We flew there on a big airplane across a really big ocean.

Here's Italy on the map. Look – it's the country shaped like a boot.

In Italy they don't speak English. They speak
Italian. I learned some important words, like
please and thank you.
Go ahead, try and say them with me.
Per favore! Grazie!
Great job!

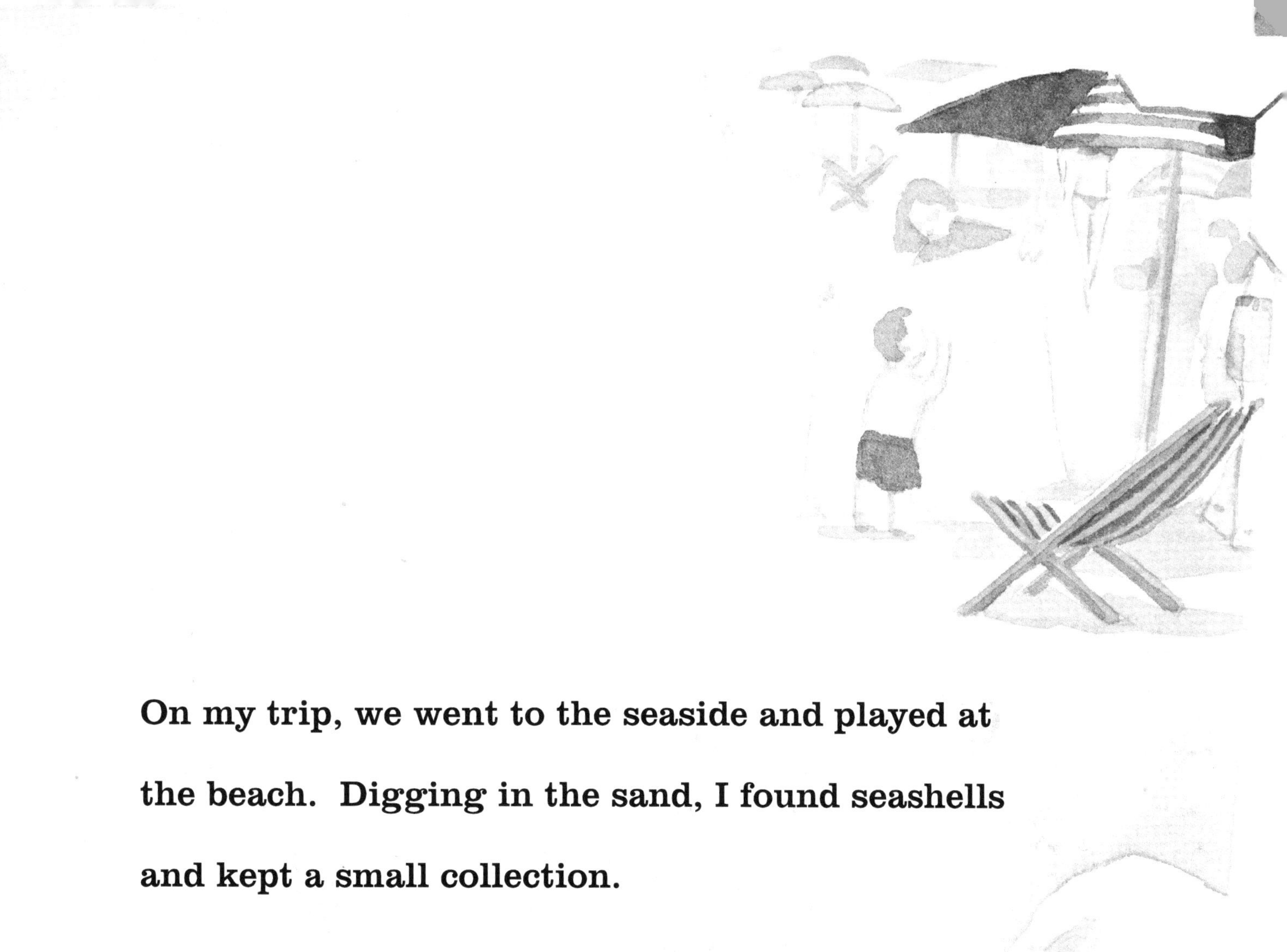

On my trip, we went to the seaside and played at the beach. Digging in the sand, I found seashells and kept a small collection.

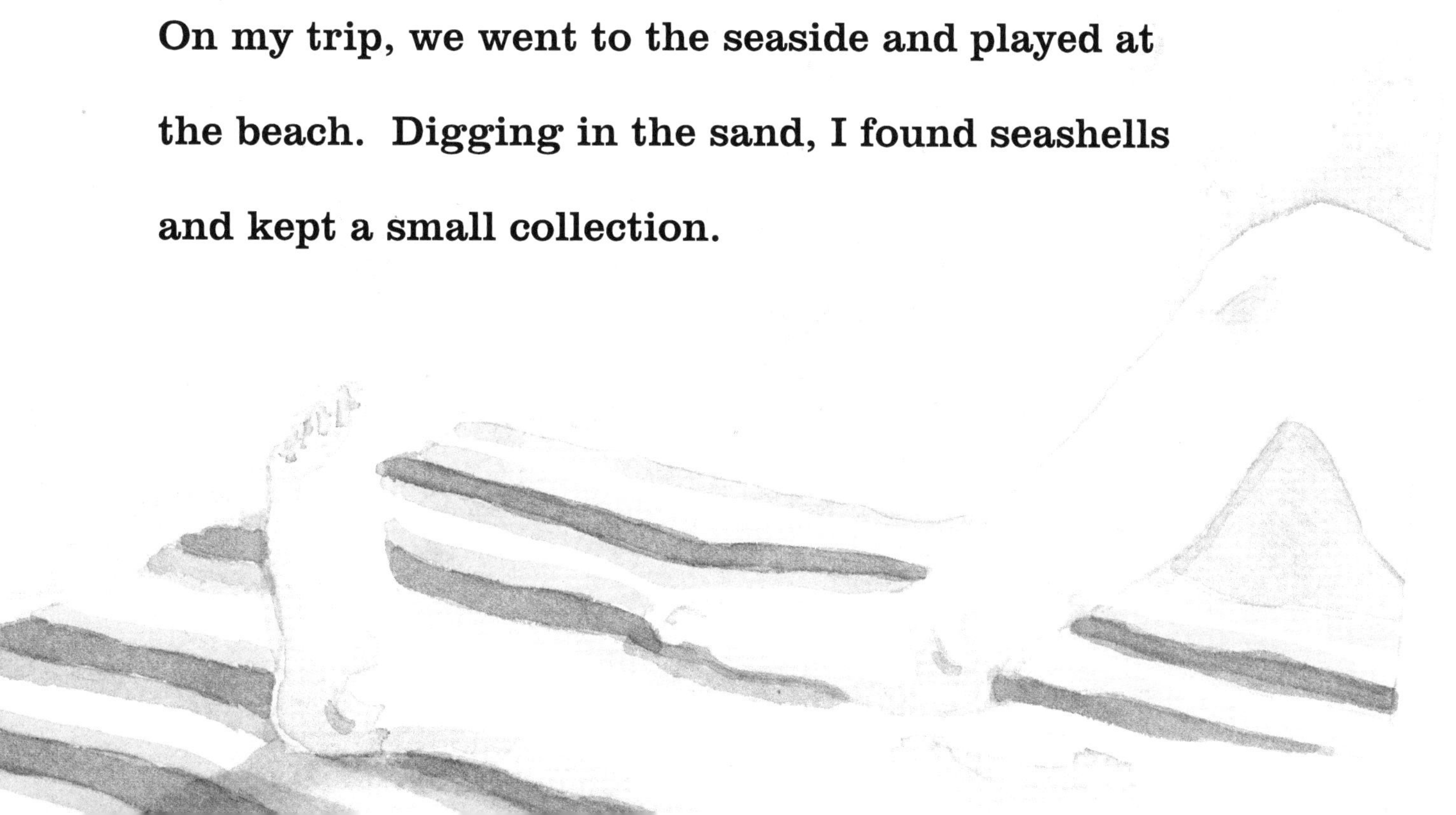

Uno
Due
Tre

Can you help me count in Italian?

Uno, due, tre, quattro, cinque. Si!

Yes! I have five seashells.

Most afternoons we played in the *piazza* or town square. In the center of the square was a huge water fountain. As the water sprayed into the air, I splashed in the fountain to cool off.

The sun's rays sparkled on the water and created a magical rainbow. I looked and looked, but never found the pot of gold.

One day we visited a farm in the countryside. A nice family lived on the farm, raising chickens and growing grapes. Their son, Giovanni, let me help with the chores.

We picked grapes and stomped on them, squirting purple juice all over us. I never knew work could be so much fun.

Italy was full of surprises. Did you know it has some of the oldest cities in the world?

We explored one ancient city that had beautiful statues and remains of old buildings called ruins.

One night we went on an underground tour and discovered a hidden city. The buildings were even older than the ones above ground. It was so dark that we needed flashlights to see.

But my favorite thing about Italy was the food.

We ate lots of pasta, pizza and ice cream.

Cioccolato
Fragola
Vaniglia

In Italy, ice cream is called *gelato*. I tried all the flavors. Every day was like a yummy birthday party. *Delizioso!* I really like Italian food.

Mommy and Daddy said we will go back to Italy soon.

Maybe you can go too!

CIAO BAMBINO! *Pronunciation and Translation Guide*

Italian Word	Pronunciation Guide	English Translation
ciao bambino	chow bahm-bee-noh	hello child
per favore	pehr fah-VOH-reh	please
grazie	GRAT-zee-eh	thank you
uno	OO-noh	one
due	DOO-eh	two
tre	treh	three
quattro	KWAHT-troh	four
cinque	CHEEN-kweh	five
sei	SEH-ee	six
sette	SEHT-teh	seven
otto	OHT-toh	eight
nove	NO-veh	nine
dieci	DYEH-chee	ten
si	see	yes
piazza	pee-AH-tsah	square
rosso	ROHS-soh	red
arancione	ah-rahn-choh-neh	orange
giallo	jahl-loh	yellow
verde	VEHR-deh	green
blu	bloo	blue
violetto	vee-oh-let-toh	violet
fantastico	fahn-TAHS-tee-koh	fantastic
gelato	jeh-LAH-toh	ice cream
cioccolato	chohk-koh-LAH-toh	chocolate
fragola	FRAH-goh-lah	strawberry
vaniglia	vah-NEEL-lyah	vanilla
delizioso	deh-lee-tsee-oh-zoh	delicious
arrivederci	ahr-ree-veh-DEHR-chee	goodbye
buon viaggio	bwon vee-ah-joh	good travels

Note to Parents

Travel provides a tremendous opportunity to expose children to different cultures at an early age. Ciao Bambino! provides the support parents need to make foreign travel easy and enjoyable. Core services include hand selected accommodations, pre-qualified childcare, equipment rental, and essential information around things like medical care and family friendly sites and activities. A successful trip is one where the parents avoid a relocation - more work in a new place - and experience a true vacation!

If you are interested in more information please visit www.ciaobambino.com or call 866-802-0300.

CIAO BAMBINO!

Printed in the United States
81766LV00003B